I Will
Love You

I Will Love You

A collection of poems
Edited by Susan Polis Schutz

Blue Mountain Press ®

P.O. Box 4549, Boulder, Colorado 80306

Library of Congress Number: 84-73378
ISBN: 0-88396-230-6

The following works have previously appeared in Blue Mountain Arts publications:

"Loving Thoughts of You," by Andrew Tawney; and "Only you . . . ," by Jamie Delere. Copyright © Blue Mountain Arts, Inc., 1983. "Our Beautiful Relationship," "Whatever I say," and "Don't be afraid," by Susan Polis Schutz. Copyright © Stephen Schutz and Susan Polis Schutz, 1984. "I love you," by Bettie Meschler; "I'm not very good at saying," by Jamie Delere; "No Matter What," by Karen Reibling; "I Love You," and "I love being," by Edward O'Blenis; "When we first met," by Rae Ellen Ditty; "You and I have seen each other," by Susan Ellington; "Nobody but You," by Laine Parsons; "I love you enough," by Nancye Sims; "You Are Loved," by Roger Pinches; "Even now," by Jeri Sweany; "I Will Love You," by Robert Stempkowski; "Every time I think of you," by Nita Daniels; "I wish," by Donna Beaupré; "I Love You," by Joshua Andrew Page; and "I Love You," by Carol A. Oberg. Copyright © Blue Mountain Arts, Inc., 1984. "We've been through rough times," by Doug Konst; "Sometimes I feel sad," by Sheryl A. Gorres; "I don't ever want to lose you . . . ," by Anna Edwards; and "All I ever need," by Shelly Roberts. Copyright © Blue Mountain Arts, Inc., 1985. All rights reserved.

Thanks to the Blue Mountain Arts creative staff.

ACKNOWLEDGMENTS appear on page 62.

Manufactured in the United States of America
Tenth Printing: November, 1998

 This book is printed on recycled paper.

Blue Mountain Press INC.

P.O. Box 4549, Boulder, Colorado 80306

CONTENTS

I Will Love You . . .

As long as I can dream,
as long as I can think,
as long as I have a memory . . .
    I will love you.

As long as I have eyes to see
and ears to hear
and lips to speak . . .
    I will love you . . .

As long as I have
    a heart to feel,
a soul stirring within me,
an imagination to hold you . . .
    I will love you.

As long as there is time,
as long as there is love,
as long as there is you,
and as long as I have a breath
    to speak your name . . .
    I will love you,
because I love
    you more
    than anything in
    all the world.

— *Daniel Haughian*

I love you
  For making each day of my life beautiful
  And all my life's labors seem worthwhile.
  For as I go through my day, no matter
  How rough it gets, I can think of you
  And smile.

I love you
  For sharing all the moments of my life
  And letting me talk, laugh and dream
  Beside you.

I love you
  For letting me speak my mind, and when
  I am through, carefully considering
  The way I feel . . .
  For letting me be myself
  And helping me to realize
  Who that really is,
  Always inspiring me to pursue
  Ideals that are lasting and real.

I love you
  For filling me with passion's desire
  And giving me more love than I
     thought
  Any person ever could.
  For making me realize my full potential
  As a person when I return your love
  The way God meant I should. . .

I love you
  For standing close when I need you,
  And standing back when I need
  To be alone, always sharing
  The sunshine and shadows of my days.
  For your comfort when I am weary,
  And your strength when the world
  Seems too much to handle.

I love you
  For all of this, and for the promise
  Of a lifetime together.
  For because of you, I have learned
  The true meaning of the words . . .
    I love you.

— *Bettie Meschler*

*Let's work slowly with each
other and build a relationship
that we both can enjoy being
a part of.*

*Let's share love and understand
that neither of us is perfect;
we are both subject to human
frailties.*

*Let's encourage each other
to pursue our dreams, even
when we're weary from trying. . .*

*Let's expect the best that
we both have to give
and still love when we fall
short of our expectations.*

*Let's be friends and respect
each other's individual personality
and give one another room to grow.*

*Let's be candid with each other
and point out strengths and
weaknesses.*

*Let's understand each other's
personal philosophy,
even if we don't agree.*

*Let's be friends
    as well as lovers.*

— Denise Braxton-Brown

I'm not very good at saying
what I need to say to you . . .
   sometimes the words don't come at all;
sometimes the tears do.
Sometimes I feel like you just
   don't understand;
sometimes I wonder if it's me.
Sometimes I wonder if we're really okay;
   sometimes your eyes tell me we are.
Sometimes I wish I could hide in your arms;
sometimes I wish you'd want to hide in mine.
Sometimes things are going great
   and I think it's here to stay;
sometimes I just have to make it through
   the day.
But sometimes . . . lots of times . . .
   I wonder what's in store for
      you and me;
and sometimes I dream
   of reaching a place in our lives
      where we could let the love
         that lives inside us
be the beautiful thing that
      I know it could be.

— Jamie Delere

No Matter What,
I Will Love You

I'm taking a chance
  caring for you . . .
I know it,
  and it scares me,
   but it won't stop me . . .
because I see too much
  in you
to just let you slip by . . .
And I've learned
  that only through
  the risks
  and the reaching out
   for more
will there ever be
 a chance for all
  I've ever dreamed.

— *Karen Reibling*

Our Beautiful Relationship

*When I was younger I dreamed
how a relationship should be
a sharing of goals
and lives
a love so strong that
it is always exciting and growing
a blending of two imperfect individuals
into stronger, better people
who laugh more, accomplish more
are happier, more successful
and more at peace . . .*

My dream came to be
because you had the same
*   dream as I*
and I want you to always know
how thankful I am
for our beautiful relationship
and how much
I love you

— *Susan Polis Schutz*

I Love You

I love you because
you are the only person
who ever got close to me
in mind, body and spirit.

I love you because
you have taught me how to
take charge of my life
through the power of first
believing in myself.

I love you because
you have made my life more
colorful, exciting and alive
by showing me that happiness . . .

isn't just being content,
it's striving toward the desire
in your heart until some part
of it has been obtained.

I love you because
you are that once-in-a-lifetime
person who has given me
that chance of a lifetime
to have a never-ending stream
of success in whatever I do.

I love you because
you are the only person
who has equally shared
in helping me grow and learn
how to live life
and live it more abundantly.

— Edward O'Blenis

*W*hen we first met, I
knew that there would
always be a special bond
between us. A bond of
warmth, closeness, love,
truth and respect. We
have come so far, through
so much, and I am proud
that the bond has not
been weakened by the
rough times, but instead
has gotten much stronger
and more loving.

— *Rae Ellen Ditty*

Until you . . .

I *never expected to feel*
   so happy
about a relationship.
I never believed I'd
experience —
   a communication so natural,
   a support so constant
   or a trust so complete.
I never imagined that by
   giving of myself,
I would be given so much more
   in return.
I never thought I could say
   "I love you" and mean it
so deeply,
as when I say it to you.

— *Paula Finn*

You and I have seen each other
at our best and our worst,
and still we remain friends.
Our love no longer depends on feelings,
but rather on a commitment of our wills
to seek only what is best for each other.

Past hurts and angry words
have not built walls between us.
Instead, they've become opportunities for us
to learn the meaning of forgiveness . . .

We've developed a mutual respect for each
    other
and a sensitivity to the needs of two
    fragile egos.

If ever you start to question what
    you mean to me,
all you need do is look into my eyes.
It's easy to see that each day
my appreciation for you
        continues to grow.

Nothing
    and no one
        will change my love for you.

— Susan Ellington

Nobody but You

I want to chase away
    any clouds you'll ever have,
and let you know
that no matter what —
    our being together
        and in love
is the most important thing
I'll ever have in this life.

When it comes to sharing love,
    today and every tomorrow,
you're the one
    that will always shine through.
And when it comes to
the person I always
        want to be with . . .
you know
    that there's
        nobody but you.

— Laine Parsons

*We've been through rough times,
and the hardest may be
yet to come.
But remember . . . the best things
in life
don't come easily.
Changes must sometimes be made,
and we must not be afraid
to make them.
For if we always remain the same,
we will fail to grow.
But if we can grow . . .
    together . . .
we will have a love
    that is known by
        so very few.*

— Doug Konst

I love you enough
that I want you to be happy.
You know better than I
what you need,
and I urge you to seek it
without fear.

I love you enough
that I want you to feel free.
I know a person must belong
to himself first,
before he can share
himself
with another . . .

I love you enough
*   to respect and accept your right*
to be the unique person you are.
The differences between us,
*   when used in a loving way,*
can be a bond that draws us
*   closer.*

I love you enough
*   that I am willing to share you*
*   with others.*
I don't ask for all of your time,
*   just some time for us*
and a place in your heart.

I love you enough
*   that I want to live with you*
*   always.*
For in you, I have what I need most,
*   and you are where I belong.*

— Nancye Sims

We have been blessed with
     each other's love and friendship.
Neither I,
          Nor any words I have
               ever written, can
express the changes you've
     wrought in my life;
The Happiness you've given me,
     Or the deep love,
          appreciation, and
               understanding I feel for you.

You asked what I would
     like to do with you?
I would like nothing more
     than to be as important to you
          as you are to me . . .

Thank you for being my lover —
   but most of all —
     for being my friend.
I trust you so completely,
   admire and appreciate
     you so much, that whatever
Time has in store for us —
   I look forward to our
     tomorrows,
   and lovingly on our
     yesterdays.

   I love you.

— Karen Hosey

*Did you know . . .
That there is no one in my world
besides you with whom I can spend
an entire day doing whatever comes
along with never a thought for anyone
else — feeling completely satisfied
because we are together?*

*Did you know . . . That there is no one
besides you whom I can talk to openly
and honestly knowing our love will only
grow and feeling a need for nothing but
our conversation?*

*Did you know . . . That there is no one
more comfortable for me than you —
whom I can enjoy silence with and never
have a need to fill the space between us
because there is no space? . . .*

Did you know . . . That no one has ever made me as happy as you have or loved me so completely — Never have I known true intimacy until we grew to where we are?

Did you know . . . That in loving you, I have experienced feelings far beyond any I could have imagined and far better than any I believed possible?

— Genevieve Bartels Wichmann

Whatever I say
means more when
you listen
Whatever I think
means more when
you understand
Whatever I do
means more when
you are there
Whatever happens to me
means more if
I can share it with you
Thank you for
adding so much
to my life

— Susan Polis Schutz

I have shared
the radiance of your smile.
I have enjoyed
the happiness of your laughter.
I have thrilled
to your slightest touch.
I have memorized
every part of you.
I have seen you say
"I love you" with your eyes.
I have learned
about life from you.
I have known
the joy of loving you
more with each passing day.
And yet,
I have only scratched
the surface of my love
            for you.

— Thomas R. Dudley

It is so bewildering
that I cannot put into words
* what you mean to me . . .*
but I think that when I hold
* you . . . silently . . .*
* it is all said.*
The first time I said,
* "I love you,"*
I was satisfied then that
* you knew,*
but the more I know you,
* the more we talk,*
* the more we share,*
I know those words are so
* inadequate.*
You are all of those beautiful,
* tender things ever said*
* . . . and much, much more.*
I don't just love you
* anymore . . .*
*   I live you.*

— Bill Lawton

I have no words I can say — none
   that will let you feel my heart
   or see my thoughts;
rather, all I can do is show you
   in what I do
that all I have — all that I am —
   is here for you.

I could search forever for words
   that would attempt to tell you
   what I have become with your
   love in my life,
but none could do.

I could search forever for words
   that would attempt to tell you
   what I wish for you,
but none could do. . .

I could search forever for words
that would attempt to tell you
what I pray for in a life ahead,
what I hope for you and me in a
world of our own choosing and
a life of our own making,
still, none could do.

So I must reduce the way I feel
into three small words,
because they are the only words
that can begin to say what is
written here . . .
"I love you."

— *Charles M. Priestap, Jr.*

*Sometimes I feel sad, and I'm
not sure if you understand why.
It's not because I'm not happy
with what we've found together.
It's not because I don't know
that you'll always care and
that you'll always be with me.
It's not even because we have to
wait awhile for our life together,
because we already share our lives.
But sometimes I just need you to
hold me and comfort me,
just to reassure me that the dream
we share is real.
And when I feel sad, it's just
my way of letting you know that
I care for you more than ever before.*

— *Sheryl A. Gorres*

I don't ever want to lose you . . .

When you are away from me
I worry sometimes that something
will happen to you —
something that might take
you away from me
I know I should only have
good thoughts
but I guess I'm just a little
insecure
I can't help but worry
because you're the best thing
that ever happened in my life
You mean everything to me . . .
and I don't ever want to lose you.

— Anna Edwards

I remember the early days
*   that we were together —*
Looking into each other's eyes,
*   smiling and shining so brightly.*

I remember the first time you
*   took my hand —*
How warm it felt, so gentle and light.
I remember the first time we held
*   each other close,*
For it was something I wanted to do
*   for so long . . .*

I remember those soft, gentle nights
        when you kept me warm.
To me it was all a distant dream
        coming true —
A bond that would last forever,
        two hearts that would dream
                together.

I remember the early days —
        our love was young, it was real.
Strong enough to last a lifetime.
A feeling that never dies
        and that no one can ever take away.

                I still love you . . .
                I always will.

                                    — Marilyn O'Keefe

You Are Loved

When the road seems too long
When darkness sets in
When everything turns out wrong
And you can't find a friend
Remember — you are loved

When smiles are hard to come by
And you're feeling down
When you spread your wings to fly
And can't get off the ground
Remember — you are loved

When time runs out before
*   you're through*
And it's over before you begin
When little things get to you
And you just can't win
Remember — you are loved . . .

When your loved ones are far away
And you are on your own
When you don't know what to say
When you're afraid of being alone
Remember — you are loved

When your sadness comes to an end
And everything is going right
May you think of your family and friends
And keep their love in sight
A thank-you for being loved

May you see the love around you
In everything you do
And when troubles seem to surround you
May all the love shine through
You are blessed — you are loved

— *Roger Pinches*

You are the best
  of all possible companions.
I love you dearly
because you accept me
for what I am, not for what
  you need or want of me.
You are the first person in my life
  who has loved me for me alone.

With you I'm not locked into a role;
I'm free to change,
  to explore and to grow.
You have shown me by your love
that I am a person of value,
and you expect from me
all that I am capable
  of accomplishing.

Thank you for being my friend,
      my love.
Thank you for insisting
that I be all that I can.
Thank you for loving me enough
  to make it all worth it.

— Judy Mason

Even now,
as many times as we have been
  together,
it is still hard for me to
  understand sometimes
just how you can keep on
    loving me.

When I get upset and angry
and say threatening things
that would make anyone else
  run the other way,
you patiently, lovingly wait
for me to pull myself together
    again.

I guess I will never really
understand the depth of your
  love for me,
but I will always accept it, and
I consider myself very fortunate
  to have you in my life.

— Jeri Sweany

All I ever need is you
to kiss away the tears
and wipe away my frowns.
All I ever need is your love
to help me through lonely nights
and to make me smile
after a long day.
All I ever need is to hear
you whisper softly
"I love you"
when I wake in the morning
and before I fall asleep at night
to make my life fully complete.

— Shelly Roberts

*I Will Love You
When We're Apart . . .*

I *missed you today;
We couldn't be together,
And I passed the time remembering
Happy yesterdays spent with you,
And anticipating many wonderful
    tomorrows.*

*I missed your smile;
That subtle yet unmistakable expression
    of your love
That melts away my doubts and fears
With its warm, unspoken reassurance,
And at the same time gives me a feeling
Of the happiness and security which only
Your deep and earnest love can give me. . .*

I missed your touch;
The gentle caresses
   that warm and soothe
Like nothing else I know.

I missed your embrace;
The loving arms that hold me still
And let the love flow freely and silently
Between us.

I missed you today;
Because you are half of all I am,
And though I could live my life alone,
Life now for me is the constant sharing
Of our thoughts and feelings,
And the unselfish sharing
Of all our lives' experiences.

— Robert Stempkowski

Every time I think of you,
I feel the sensation again . . .
of loving you
and missing you like you
could never imagine.
What I want more than anything
right now is to hold you
in my arms
and tell you
just how much I love you
and how much
I want you in my life.

Please . . . don't ever doubt
my love for you . . .
because it is as real today
as it was
the day we first
began to share a love.

— *Nita Daniels*

*Sometimes late at night
I think of the color of your eyes
when you laugh*

*And the tilt of your head
when you listen*

*And I remember the warmth
of your touch
when we are close*

*In the darkness of those nights
I see you in my mind
and I can feel the love we share*

*And I know we are special
and that our love will endure.*

— Jennifer Sue Oatey

Loving Thoughts of You

It's all your fault, you know . . .
I've hardly accomplished
anything today.
Every time I begin something,
you creep into my thoughts —
softly, slowly at first . . .

and before I know it,
my imagination is filled
with thoughts of you.
Warm thoughts,
nice thoughts,
such loving thoughts.

But this is getting out of hand,
and I have to get something
done today.
So maybe I'll begin
by doing something
very important . . .

I'll let you know
how much I want you
how much I need you
and how
very much
I love you.

— Andrew Tawney

I wish
that for just one moment
you
could be me
just so you could know
how much
I
love
you.

— *Donna Beaupré*

*I love being your friend and lover —
doing little things to brighten
  your life
and watching you burst into a warm
smile that says, "Thank you for being
  you!"
But what I like most is how you and
  I have fallen in love —
There are no demands, no using each
  other,
just letting those wonderful feelings
  continue to grow . . .
And in return, finding that being
friends and lovers at the same time
  is a rich and rewarding experience.*

— Edward O'Blenis

I Love You

*These past few years, I suppose
we've changed as often as the seasons.
But there has always been a rainbow
at the end of each storm, a calm
that seems to last as long as we're
together.*

*I've been alone. I've paced my steps
over and again, but never once have
you left my thoughts. You're always
with me.*

*We've been through a lot. We've grown
in pain; we've been stretched far
beyond love's boundaries. Yet
there has never been a time that our
arms weren't open wide for refuge.*

*To me, you're the peace that calms
my windy days and brings about spring
in the heart of every frozen winter.
I adore you, and my love for you
is forever.*

— Joshua Andrew Page

Don't be afraid
to love someone
totally and completely
Love is the most fulfilling
and beautiful feeling in the world
Don't be afraid that you will
get hurt
or that the other person
won't love you as much
There is a risk in
everything you do
and the rewards
are never so great
as what love can bring
So let yourself get involved
completely and honestly
and enjoy the possibility
that what happens
might be the only real
source of happiness

— Susan Polis Schutz

I Love You

If I had to count the ways I love you,
the numbers would stretch around this
world but never end.
If I had to speak or write to explain
my love for you,
my voice would grow hoarse trying,
my hand become numb,
and my mind frustrated with its
inadequacies. . .

But one of the miracles of this love
I have for you is that it needs
no counting,
no explanations,
no play of eloquent words.
What counts is that you know it exists,
that it lives without explanation when
we are apart, temporarily distracted,
or silent.
That when I say, "I love you,"
it is sincere,
straight from the heart,
and of the kind that will not end.
I love you.

— Carol A. Oberg

Only You . . .

A lot of people know the surface side of me,
the side they see while I'm working
or just going through the day . . .
But there's another side of me — an inside —
that people never see.
It's a part that's full of a thousand thoughts,
a part that embraces love and cherishes friendship,
a part that understands without need for words,
a part that has yearnings and desires and prayers . . .

The inside of me has so many moods
that the outside never shows.
For once in my life, though . . .
I trust someone implicitly
and I care about someone in a totally
    understanding way.
I feel like it's okay to let that someone in . . .
to let them see me emotionally
and physically
as naturally and as naked as I can be.
I have given myself to you
and told you things that
I've never told another soul.

You are the one person who has seen me
trembling and as fearful as an injured bird;
you are the one person I always want
to take with me when I feel
exhilarated and my spirits are soaring.

I trust you with my secrets,
and you now know that
    you can trust me with yours.
This sharing . . . this special sharing . . .
is one of the nicest dimensions
                my life has ever known.

— Jamie Delere

ACKNOWLEDGMENTS

We gratefully acknowledge the permission granted by the following authors, publishers and authors' representatives to reprint poems and excerpts from their publications.

Daniel Haughian for "I Will Love You." Copyright © Daniel Haughian, 1984. All rights reserved. Reprinted by permission.

Denise Braxton-Brown for "Let's work slowly." Copyright © Denise Braxton-Brown, 1983. All rights reserved. Reprinted by permission.

Paula Finn for "Until you . . . " Copyright © Paula Finn, 1983. All rights reserved. Reprinted by permission.

Karen Hosey for "We have been blessed." Copyright © Karen Hosey, 1983. All rights reserved. Reprinted by permission.

Genevieve Bartels Wichmann for "Did you know . . ." Copyright © Genevieve Bartels Wichmann, 1983. All rights reserved. Reprinted by permission.

Thomas R. Dudley for "I have shared." Copyright © Thomas R. Dudley, 1984. All rights reserved. Reprinted by permission.

Bill Lawton for "It is so bewildering." Copyright © Bill Lawton, 1983. All rights reserved. Reprinted by permission.

Charles M. Priestap, Jr. for "I have no words." Copyright © Charles M. Priestap, Jr., 1985. All rights reserved. Reprinted by permission.

Marilyn O'Keefe for "I remember the early days." Copyright © Marilyn O'Keefe, 1985. All rights reserved. Reprinted by permission.

Judy Mason for "You are the best." Copyright © Judy Mason, 1985. All rights reserved. Reprinted by permission.

Jennifer Sue Oatey for "Sometimes late at night." Copyright © Jennifer Sue Oatey, 1985. All rights reserved. Reprinted by permission.